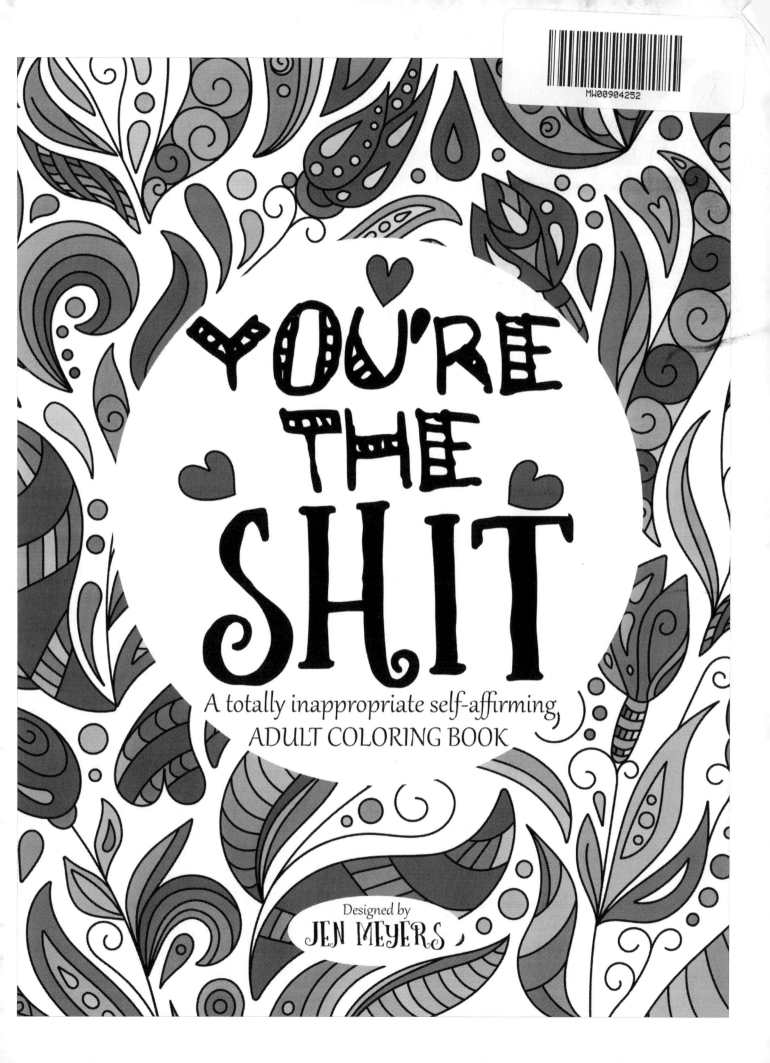

The Totally Inappropriate Coloring Books:

YOU'RE THE SHIT
YOU'RE TOTALLY BADASS
YOU ARE ONE BAMF
F♥CK CANCER*

*(a portion of the proceeds donated to research dedicated to finding a cure for cancer)

Please Note: This books contains adult language and is not intended for children.

Published in May 2016 by Turning Leaves Press, Inc.

Artwork © Andriy Lipkan, Irinakrivoruchko, Antimartina, Ratselmeister, Mariia Brzhezinskaia, Somjai Jaithieng, Lidiya Krutykh-Amelina, Tatiana Gorohova, Pe3ak, Memoru, Galyna Novykova, Ipanki, Frescomovie, Anna Lezhepekova, Alexander Pokusay, Alexandra Vertysheva, Lilipom10 :: www.dreamstime.com

ISBN 978-1533001566

WELCOME!

This coloring book was designed to entertain—to make you smile, laugh, and feel good about yourself. What could be more enjoyable and stress-reducing than coloring? How about when some of the coloring pages include cheekily profane (yet positive) messages? Because, let's face it, sometimes it makes all the difference when someone tells you that you're the shit. (You are, by the way.) Regardless of whether those exact words (or more socially acceptable ones) are used, everyone needs to hear that kind of thing from time to time. Even from the pages of a coloring book.

So...

If you're stressed or depressed, this is the coloring book for you.

If you get all sweary sometimes, this is the coloring book for you.

If you are someone who appreciates a fan-fucking-tastically profane turn of phrase, this is the coloring book for you.

If you don't swear around your children/co-workers/clients but have ALL THE SWEARS bouncing off the walls of your brain, this is the coloring book for you.

If you are, however, easily offended by vulgar language...this is probably NOT the coloring book for you. (But even if this isn't your cup of tea, I still think you're the shit. And I bet you know someone who'd be ALL over this kind of thing. I mean, don't we all?)

I have been a fan of coloring FOREVER, and am thrilled that you've picked up my creation. I hope this book brings you joy, and that you get all the happy feels as you color the shit out of it.

Happy coloring!

Inappropriately yours,

JEN

P.S. If you like this book, there are more Totally Inappropriate coloring books available: *You're TOTALLY Badass, You are One BAMF,* and *F*ck Cancer* (a portion of the proceeds from the cancer coloring book is being donated to support research dedicated to finding a cure for cancer. Because fuck cancer.)

you ARE a

SPECIAL
fucking snowflake

Don't ever
fucking
change

you've got this

YOU MATTER

in every fucking way

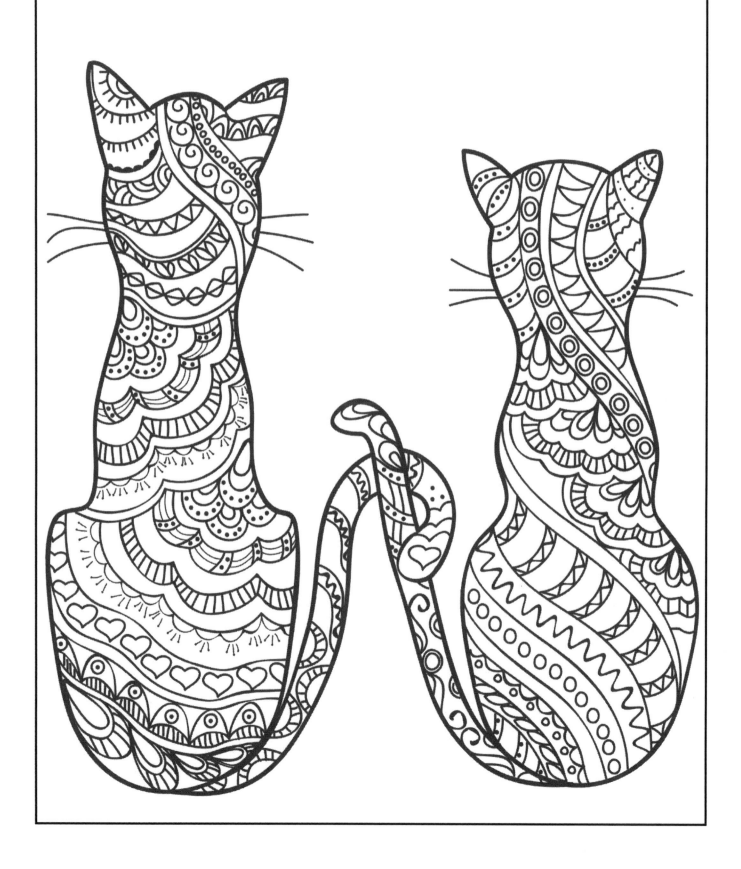

You have a tribe

and they're fucking awesome

JUST LIKE YOU

NO
BULLSHIT

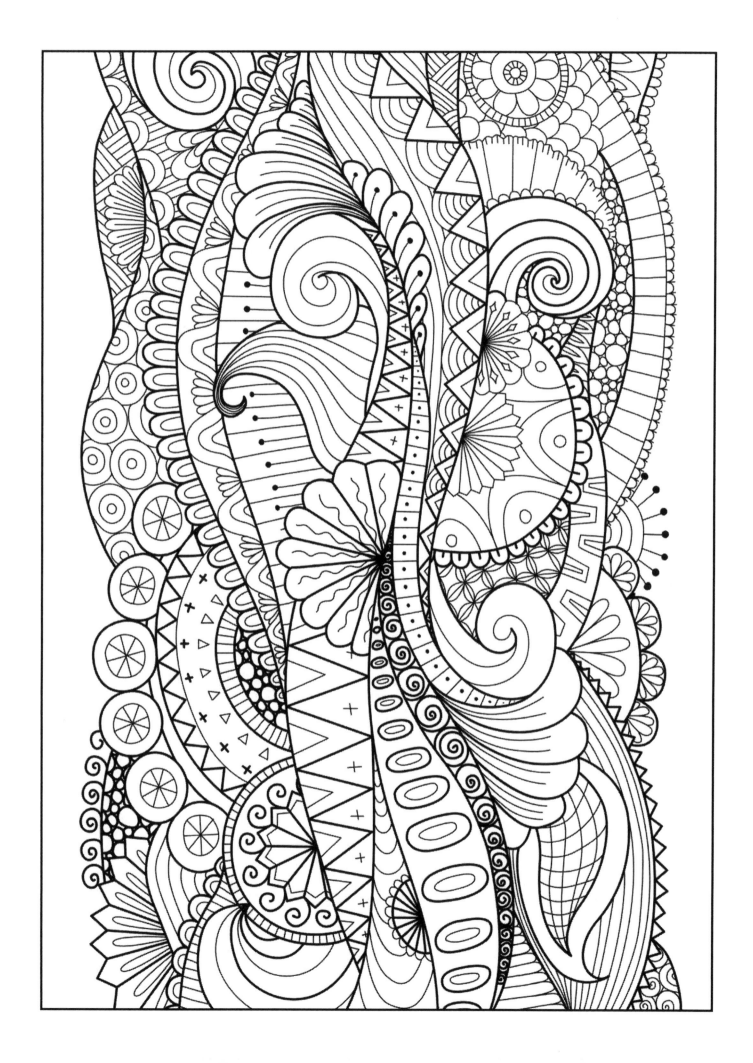

Thank You!

I totally think you're the shit for picking up this book, and I truly hope you enjoyed it. If you did, would you be so kind as to post a review wherever you purchased it? And please don't be a stranger! Drop me a line at jen@jmeyersbooks.com or visit me on Facebook at www.facebook.com/jmeyersbooks. I'm also on Twitter and Instagram as @jmeyersbooks.

Hope to meet you soon!
JEN

JEN MEYERS grew up in Vermont, spent three years in Germany when she was a kid, and now lives in central New York. When she's not reading, writing, or designing coloring books, she's chasing after her four kids, playing outside, relishing the few quiet moments she gets with her husband, and forgetting to make dinner.

Besides designing Totally Inappropriate coloring books, she also writes contemporary romance and young adult fantasy. She is the author of the (completely appropriate) *Intangible* series, the (perfectly inappropriate) *Happily Ever After* series and *Anywhere*, and co-author of the (totally inappropriate) *Untamed* series. For more information about Jen and her work, visit her website www.jmeyersbooks.com.

Made in the USA
Middletown, DE
30 June 2017